Write the Vision:

A Journey to Forgiveness in Poems
and Other Celebrations

Write the Vision:

A Journey to Forgiveness in Poems
and Other Celebrations

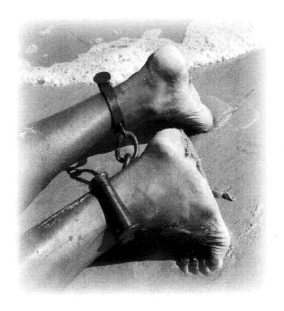

Benjamin Edgar Williams

authorHOUSE®

AuthorHouse™
1663 Liberty Drive
Bloomington, IN 47403
www.authorhouse.com
Phone: 1-800-839-8640

Published by AuthorHouse   10/16/2012

ISBN: 978-1-4772-5455-4 (sc)
ISBN: 978-1-4772-5456-1 (hc)
ISBN: 978-1-4772-5457-8 (e)

Library of Congress Control Number: 2012913860

Contents

This work is dedicated to my mothers:

Frances; she gave me life and love

Joyce; she gave me hope and vision

Irene; she gave me joy and a dream

Acknowledgements

Thank you Elliott, my youngest son, for your assistance, patience and tolerance of me telling you where and how to point the camera and get the shots of my legs in shackles. I couldn't have done it without you. Kyra, my eldest, you are an inspiration to me with a courage that I would do well to emulate. Brent there is nothing you cannot do with the energy and determination you possess. Tyrease, though the winds of life have been a storm without equal I admire that you still stand. Kelsey I wish I could write as well as you. The world will soon know your talent.

And

Thank you, Eleanor Rose Daniels, for being my first true love. You left us much too soon. I'll love you always. Rest in Peace

Preface
Write the vision

Alone, I arrived on a deserted beach, washed from an angry sea. I was beaten. I was bruised and injured. On my knees, my lungs fought in contest with water and air. I expelled the water. Laboring to my feet, I became aware of my tattered clothes, the taste of bile and salt, and searing pain rising from my ankles. I felt weight. I was bound by shackles—fettered and restrained. The question of *why*, like a mist, fogged my thoughts. However, in the next moment, my eyes caught purchase of a view of the land. In my gaze were lush hills, fertile valleys, and majestic peaks. It seemed good to get there. I attempted to journey. My ankles made immediate protest and my chains cried out in whimsical agreement. *Why?* returned. I spoke the question aloud, and my tears became bound by sand. On my knees again, I felt the warmth of a hand encouraging me to stand. I saw no one. I wasn't afraid, and my heart seemed rested. Again, I entreated, *Why?*

To my heart, the messenger asked, "Would you be free?" I didn't understand, but responded, "Yes." In the most penetrating thought that undid almost all my argument, the messenger said, "Forgive." My response was not immediate. I held my peace and momentarily embraced my captivity. This place of pain was familiar and, like my chains, could be tolerated. I recounted the solitude of my surroundings. I considered my current station as a place framed by spectacular views and yet only a few feet from my past. Again, the messenger queried, "Would you be free?" This time, I answered honestly, "I don't know." I felt sadness as I heard the messenger depart. I still did not see anyone but sensed the load of labored footfalls in a distance. In the same instance, my ankles began to burn with more pain than I remembered. The sea was moving back for me. Gradually, the sea overcame the earth on which I stood and I wanted to cry out. In the next moment, whether of panic or desperation, my lungs forced out my cry, "I DON'T KNOW HOW TO FORGIVE; HOW DO I LET GO OF THE PAIN?" Lament and anguish forced me down, but my knees didn't reach the sand. A hand and a hairy arm stopped me. I saw a man. I saw his feet. He had scars on his ankles. His voice was different from the one that had told me to forgive. He said, "Let me show you."

Alone, I arrived . . .

On *Thursdays* and the days that follow

I once read that we have so little control of our lives. I tend to agree. Our hair color, eye color, nationality, race, birthplace, parents, and day of arrival into this continual play are predetermined. Our ability to choose—the freedom we guard with unyielding devotion, that right that we enjoin as a coming of age—is diluted to little more than an agreement to perform within the limitations of our script. I believe, for the most part, that we rehearse behaviors modeled by our mommas and daddies and their deficiencies, which were impacted by their mommas and daddies. We perform, produce, and move to hit our "marks," as directed, in our arenas and stages of life.

It is interesting that we are called *offspring*. This, I believe, unravels a truth. In time, we are launched and bounce into tracks of conformity or rebellion, which tear at us, in an effort to prevent the past and its inherent curses.

Many of our choices, unveiled, are not choices at all, but responses . . .

I was born on a Thursday, as was my father, my eldest daughter, and my oldest and youngest sons . . .

I was born *of* Compton, California. I'm a son, produced from love, nurtured by the conflicts of pain and pleasure. I honor my ascendants—my father, maternal and paternal grandfathers—with my pseudonym, Benjamin Edgar Williams.

As I have walked, run, fought, fled, stood, stumbled, fallen, and continued to stand again, one constant has remained apparent: I'm still here. My mystery and quest has been to determine *why*.

The question persists, and the answer is not always clear, but sometimes, when I am still, I start to move through the cloud. Unfortunately, stillness is rare and far too infrequent and comes when confronted by insurmountable mountains, impassable walls, crevasses, and raging torrents. As I age, I understand that some of these circumstances stop me by design. Then, those moments of pause are beyond argument, and after the anger, frustrations, despair, and denial retreat, the unrelenting voice of my calling is intelligible and distinct.

Writing is my calling. Writing not only gives me voice but also answers the cry that is a deep perpetual chord within me. It is my music and the instrumentation to my play. It is my connection to the eternal—to God.

I am a writer of prose, a poet, and a playwright. *Write the Vision* is the first verse of my movement. I trust it finds harmony with your spirit.

Bound by shackles . . .

Fragile Flowers
(cry of an abused child)

Wind whips the petals;

> See them blow.

No pain, still cried in silence,

> Don't you *NO?*

THERE colors, still resilient,

> Like the show?

C'mon time, stop the progress,

> Let 'em go!

Child looks, the bruises fountain,

> Have your way.

Perfect skin mends broken bones;

> Hurt, you say?

Climbing out, the *WHOLE* behind,

> Seized in day.

Oh, the fragile flowers grow.

                    Watch the play!
Fragile flowers in beauty sun.

                    Smell the scent.
Rooting deep in *LEAVES*, they thrive,

                    Feel the bent.
Petals fall, the flowers fail,

                    Relief or went?
Redeem the clay, her flowers seed,

                    Life extent.
In childhood blooms, **there** flowers bud,

                    Sun comes fast.
Broken wind, breaks air and *PIECE*

                    How will they last?

My Heart Speaks to You

What can I create or build or shape,

What gift or jewels can I bring?

How soft can I touch or tender words,

To quiet scorched memory's sting.

We looked and we shared, and kisses we made,

Embraced by love entwined.

I knew your love, but then to doubt—

True hearts bosomed cries and binds.

Much simply put in words so few,

Teared voicing speaks my heart.

I wronged your love and wounded souls,

And I fear the span, the part.

When bridges build and travel joined,

Can reach your heart's far shores,

I will find dance, and sing new songs,

When God, new life, restores.

Quiet Tears

They have no sound, when falling down,
To hit the seams of light.
They fall around, seem upside down,
And wrench my soul in flight.

I call to you, find some to do,
Of things just left inside.
It still feels hurt of some strange worth,
But sound, itself, has died.

Can things undone and time so long
Tend wounds on boyish holes?
Will waves retreat and dry hurt's feet,
Attend and mend my soul?

I hear you, Dad, and feel the sad,

Of times and questions lost.

Your voice hits deep and comes replete,

Makes questions of parents' cost.

I need you now, to show, tell how,

These things, my insides out.

Help sell the pain, stop, hold the drain,

Arrest and traverse mount.

I hold my hand and hope to plan,

To make these things that bend.

Come time, and die, and time's new eye,

I'll have my Dad again.

So tell me, Dad, of what you had,

Was I of special note?

Can pride constrain or striving vain,

Have stood with me to gloat?

My days will past, I'll never last,

To have and make time again.

This way will end, time never has

'nough answers to next, begin.

Teach Me

I am a difficult animal to understand. I am a man. I am strong, proud, assured, but lacking in so much. I lack that part, that piece, that skill that is not perfected in me until I am willing to give it totally away—my love, myself. "Me," that selfish being of oneness, is at the very core of my being, but it yearns for something it does not know or understand. It just knows. Meanwhile, I have guarded "me" and protected him from injury and wounds that I experience (both real and imagined). The layers are deep and made solid by my years—years that have seen trauma and failure. I've told myself that I treasure "me" and swear an allegiance to protect "me" at all cost. However, "me" cannot remain a prisoner. That is not His design or intent and yet, at times I trouble my own soul with my fierce tenacity of will that keeps "me" to myself.

If I continue cloistered by my stubbornness, I will forever be alone and incomplete unless I give "me" away and love more than myself.

What I Learned Today

If all the world told me that they love me,

it is of little worth

because the most meaningful love of me has diminished . . .

mine.

I've got to find it, feel it, and know it . . .

Then, my eyes
caught purchase of a
view . . .

I Need to Ask You Something

(for Irene)

I need to ask you something, Momma.

How do I get hands like yours?

Hands that touch and try to heal,

Hands that hold and always feel,

Hands that help and wipe the tears,

Hands that cradled, oh, the years.

How do I get hands like yours?

I need to ask you something, Momma.

How do I get eyes like yours?

Eyes that saw these treasures in time,

Eyes that see the children in prime,

Eyes that told in growing old,

Eyes that told their journeyed souls.

How do I get eyes like yours?

I need to ask you something, Momma.

How do I get ears like yours?

Ears that hear of future winds,

Ears that know things come again,

Ears that listen when babies pine,

Ears that blended the joys of time.

How do I get ears like yours?

I need to ask you something, Momma.

How do I get a nose like yours?

A nose that sensed things out of place,

A nose that knew a child's disgrace,

A nose that bore the smells of youth,

A nose appreciated, a nose of use.

How do I get a nose like yours?

I need to ask you something, Momma.

How do I get a tongue like yours?

A tongue that knew and sought to taste,

A tongue that tried and found a place,

A tongue that stilled, held **kept** and **kept** quiet,

A tongue that laughs, its constant diet.

How do I get a tongue like yours?

And finally, Momma, I need to ask you something.

Who did you see to trust in Jesus?

How did you speak and hear from God?

Where were you when he touched your purpose?

What were the tastes on this road you've trod?

Momma,

      When time calls and holds my hand,

      I hope I can go, I hope I can stand.

      My joy, my hope, my heart's desire,

      To sense and act as you've inspired.

I Dreamed of You

I saw my children standing, shoulders high and eyes in focus.

Justice was in their mouths and at their feet, lay oppression docile.

They were master of no man, only servants of God-inspired destinies.

These strong children of mine suffered the crucible, the chastening of discipline, and now understood wisdom.

Knowledge was their captive.

These strong children of mine had not perfect skin or soft brows.

Their hands were not tender and their gaits were not feeble.

They had companioned pain and trial and had suckled at breast made bitter, yet they grew strong.

Their perfection born of endurance and zeal made complete in the fire.

Their compassionate embrace arrived in knowing tears and melding its salt into their souls.

I Wish for You
(for Kelse)

Of filled days, health, wealth, and much joy,
Sincerest of feelings with first kiss from a boy.
A doll, bouncing puppies, you treasured as toys.
Someday, baby's face, smiled, pleasured and coy.

With you I have treasure, wealth, health, and pure joy.
A baby no longer, eyes widened and coy,
God's grace gave you dollies and puppies, your toys.
I look, long, and wonder what man grows your boy.

Hard times, yes, are fleeting and good times give pause,
They both give us memories and mark roads with cause.
Time tells us how life was, and light's subtle clause,
No rerun, no replay, no challenge life's flaws.

So hear my appeal, sweet, and mold questions too.
How long will you live and what build you your view?
Of things that will falter, wear down and change hue?
Find love in your treasure; you'll always be new.

In the light

In the light,

    the obvious is apparent

    the reflections are clear

    the sounds are distinct

    and the languages are formed and articulated

In the light,

    your eyes sing in celebration

    your lips press with urgency

    your ears time your pulse

    and your unrehearsed moves respond from memory

In the light,

    I kiss, hold, and squeeze your heart

    I fondle, cajole, and invite your passions

    I cradle, caress, and captivate your seasons

    and I speak words silently into your being

In the light,

    we find ourselves and learn love

    we sought pleasures and fought our souls

    we look to places and wonder their direction

    and we accept the peace of passing time

the Cost of a Kiss

What lingers on your tongue
And blushes your cheeks?
Turning and tingeing,
Finding flesh to make red.

Lips that purse, then open,
Receiving and accepting
Time and tenderness
And warmth that floods.

In exchange for passions,
Wanton lust or real,
Questions cost, its investment
Made in heart's payments.

Consider now, the value,

The cost and its expense.

Timed-treasured moments

Spent and not returned.

A kiss not complete

Love enjoined in passion

Requite with touch and taste

Make joy its attending.

Touch my heart, as I

Feel tensions released and more.

Finish the lush union

Join fervor and fever.

Kiss and cost for nothing.

No payment could find

Tongued deeply half rhythms

Cost could doubt complete.

Ask Me (for Beautiful)

Ask me why I love you

And I will tell your eyes

Of visions and journeys seen

And hope that tells the prize

Ask me why I love you

And I will take your hand

Hold gently to my breast

Feel heart that beats the plan

Ask me why I love you

And I will hold you near

Speak volumes in fragrant words

With kisses upon your ear

Ask me why I love you

And I will bring you time

As witness and our disciple

Our treasure possessed in rhyme

Ask me why I love you

And I will reach to God

Find way and battle thwarted

Our footfalls still to trod

Ask me why I love you

And I will wipe your tears

Bear heart and soul with passion

Our mind, without its fears

Ask me why I love you

Simply put, love calls to me

A life without you, empty

Fulfilled with you, are we

Would you be free?

Seasons

Time is funny,

not that it sets out to construct a rhyme with humorous results . . .

but it is capricious in its delivery of sage devices, plans, and

instructions . . .

for without "our" requisition or desire these "instructions" arrive.

Their timing seems to be of no consequence in the moment but . . .

after the flames die down and the cinders are sifted, do we really

find the seed of the crucible . . .

Heal, dear child, heal . . . this has been marked on the calendar of your life.

It has not been an accident because God was not asleep. He knew this day would come, and He is here. In His arms you are destined for rest and resolve.

Be His child today. His hands will bear your tears and will not forget.

I will not forget either.

My Prayer

When I lay at night to rest,

I pray my Lord, I've done my best,

And if I die, I'll journey blessed,

To have lived and held you at my chest.

When . . .

When all is said

And today we read

And all is pulled apart

the Day will rest

We'll have our best

And echoes claim our heart

When we lie down

When we lie down

I talk with you

I hear your face

I see traces on your skin

You tell my ear

"I miss you dear,"

"I wondered where you've been."

When we lie down

When we lie down

You move your toes

I call your face

You cradle your neck in me

We calm and clown

It's too far down

There are tigers in the sea

When we lie down

When we lie down

You save this song

And ask yourself

When you are in my heart

What words you've said

That touched my head

The love, the music, start.

When we lie down

When we lie down

Forgive . . .

Two Thoughts

When two thoughts met two truths,

Engaged with passion's heat,

Two times were measured by two pasts,

And traveled different seats.

When two thoughts spoke two truths,

And hearing moved in vain,

Their two times marked two pasts;

No hearing was made plain.

When two thoughts stopped two truths,

And empathy was missed,

Now two thoughts scored two pasts

As injuries, after bliss.

What of two thoughts and hear two truths,

To banquet err in trance.

Try two thoughts and seek two pasts,

And partner in the dance.

If

If only you still listened,
When days had been a wear,
If only you, my vision,
I see, alone, I stared.

If only words had softened,
And your hand still plied my brow,
If only your arms built safety,
And led me back to now.

If only life kissed and sweetened,
And filled me, hope instilled,
If only we'd raised love's fire,
And passion, still we build.

If only you carried joyful,

And brought him to our flame,

If only time's no passage,

I'd ever extol your name.

If only pain's no partner,

No claim, no door to us,

If perfect rise and sunset,

No end, love's plan and trust.

Then we'll see our love rise,

Unfettered of time and space,

And I will gaze your beauty,

'Till my time, this life, erase.

A few feet from my
past,

New Shoes, No Feet

There is a walk of lilt, a dance, a step,

A way of distinction, of confidence, of pep.

But woe there the man, the woman, the girl,

With *Prada* and *Gucci,* but no toes to curl.

Come! What be the sight, the question, the clues,

Hear versed sad trauma, "No feet, but new shoes."

T'was focus, not aim 'caused physical err,

Left sad, the cripple, skewed hope, and bone bare.

Her feet bore the challenge, his feet held the clue,

In arms, held their strength, their eyes held a view.

They stumbled; they fell, headlong and entwined,

Immobiled, infirmed, *incisioned,* not kind.

Parted limbs, bloodied portions, deformed, made confused,

Unable to move, embittered, felt used.

Memory's motions, impassioned with thoughts fleet of foot

Unable, not willing, to station, or root . . .

Then tomorrows will come with yesterday's glue.

Crying, 'fear for the moment,' inviting the shoe.

But bearing's the hardest when standing's forsook,

And standing's impossible with new shoe, no foot.

Who cut off your hand, its limb after leg?

And stopped peace in process, its torrent, its segue?

Will time heal emotions, yes pure and atone,

But how mend, how fasten, this heel to its home?

"I don't know how to forgive!"

fifty 8

50 eight

fifty 8

born to die

roads to march and

come by

passing, sometimes looking

    taking a glance

        thinking a chance

           will come

Time passes

never looking back

    not stopping

        not waiting

No acknowledgment

    not even hi or any other greeting

I exist

remembered by . . .

those | touch

those | hurt

the tears recorded

they etched

they sketched

and kept score

Did | win?

Did the game count?

| kept calling for time . . .

looked for officials

STOP the game!

STOP the play!

JUST STOP!

|'m tired.

so tired.

it doesn't slow down . . .

if you stop you die.

Momma died at 58.

Daddy died before her, but kept playing.

his game was well rehearsed and

        his muscle kept him animated.

He played as a master athlete

he sat down after the show

                  and watched

      his wife was embraced

        his body held on

           his mind found purchase

then his muscle weakened

      and the bond escaped.

Daddy left the ballpark

           with his ball and bat

I watched

      tears bathed me . . .

        finding dirt . . .

          making mud . . .

           it dried . . .

some flaked.

Meanwhile, doesn't seem enough.

The game continues,

no bench-warming

no hoping Daddy sees my hit

remembered his stroke, his swing

He doubted me

my metal, my muscle

my meat.

I don't.

I watched.

Learning happened . . .

but how long will I have to play . . .

past 58?

I hope so.

What Next, God?

My mirror looks back at me and laughs.

Wretched man, can't stand the image that I see,

When will my time come?

How will I know?

I can't tell the seasons without looking at the sun,

Can't tell my troubles to go until their time has come,

Can't change the way I see,

Can't change inside of me,

Who can?

I fight, I struggle

I scream and cry.

I climb, I fall

I build and fail.

Sometimes I think I'll break.

I want to die.

Instead I just cry.

Out to you, my Lord.

What next, God?

What next?

When does my path begin to climb?

I want to go up;

I'm tired of down.

When will it come?

When will it come?

When will it come?

What If I Ask?

Hear war inside today,

Don't know if, or how to fight.

It seems such contradiction—

To run, to study, or write.

How challenge I the futures,

Of creative versus real.

It wars against my spirit,

I threaten not to feel.

Inside, I feel the baffles

Open, close and flowing through.

I see the softened voices,

That beg stop to hear the view.

Shall ask the sage of wisdom?

Bring focus, calm the noise.

How deafen raging warriors;

Send quiet, return with joys.

And yet the warriors clamor—

Scream shouts and mount demands—

I choose not acquiescence.

I climb to rock; I stand

Must gain a vantage, a standpoint

Against the rage of beast.

Escape their reach, their footpath,

Find solace in the least.

Where gifts arrive in secret,

Implanted, carried. *wombed*

Unchallenged, never growing,

Some jailed and there entombed.

Release, cries voice of wisdom.

Develop, grow my prize

Help fruit to feed the hungry;

Help voice to all that cry.

Help speak, obey commission:

My charter and His decree.

Help write as though I live,

Help my spirit to be free.

"Let me show you how."

Today

When time had set its course
And seasons developed hues,
Then fountains became "in-motions"
Where raindrops compelled the dew.

I saw embraced in heart-strings
And heard your humbled cry;
We touched and silence broken,
Words watered where visions die.

I called, you quickly answered,
Told all of worlds unseen,
Believed and raised my failings,
Spoke light to heal my dreams.

How can I match your faith?
Or reach to raise our mind?
Find payment, complete your circle,
Remit and breech the bind.

Would love attend its calling?
Bring camphor to the wound?
How heal in chambered struggle,
Give flight embittered tombs.

Mine eye does see its challenge,
Conceive the call to span.
I sojourn the more in memory,
Than feet allow, I stand.

Release, I cry to footpaths,
You see the path I go.
Alas, I have no challenge,
Save memory, broken soul.

Wherein is all my clamor?
My roar, my beast, my scream?
I fear my waking visions
And question real and dream.

For this I put in poem
To love, I say of thee,
Sorrow for still disrupted,
Requite, redeem, re-me.

These Hands

If you look at my hands
You'd see nothing extra special.
They are complete with digits that have been worn with time.
Deep furrows carve my palm,
And shallow scars grace the other side.
There is little fat embedded across my fingers,
And yet the protrusion of veins outlines my grasp.
They are hands that have clenched tight in anger and dared
blood to approach my fingers' tips.
They are hands that have contoured, cradled, and supported
heads, feet, backs, and shoulders,
Attending to its own wounds and then sometimes to others.'
They have pooled tears and fought cries.
They have petitioned clarity in moments of exclamation.
Then they had pleaded to God and fingered the devils.
They hold on to the invisible,

reach back for past wisdom,

and beckon a coming future . . .

all the while remembering to stoop to help.

These hands are nothing extra special,

But they're all I have.

I am grateful for every pain, pleasure, ache, excitement, chill,

warmth, burn, and scar.

They are my hands, and with them I can touch my world.

Just Thinking

I thought:

Notes from the desk of . . .

Quotes from the best of . . .

Dotes from the rest of . . .

Votes from the crest of . . .

Then said:

When hell hath filled its final space,

And seats above are quenched by grace,

Then chairs beside the standing race

Will cry the tear of fallen face.

And did:

Moved time and shoved space,

Shushed thunder and scolded lightening,

Bottled oceans and poured rivers,

Made babies and taught them to cry.

Simple rules:

Speak the truth

Look for honesty

Hear innocence

Savor that which is good

Appreciate sugar for sugar's sake

to touch as a child

there is a tenderness that a child knows,

that some of us have forgotten.

it is honest and unpretentious, pure and unfettered:

it requires that we touch . . .

because of love,

unafraid to be rejected . . .

willing to move beyond self and become naked and

vulnerable . . .

this is the best way to love.

this is the best way to be loved.

this love cannot be found because it's not lost,

it's in us.

It is a decision, a choice, a will . . .

time and desire are the forces that *can* move us to remember . . .

and try again.

You've Taken My Hand

The journey began with a touch, a smile, with grace in your eyes and warmth on your lips. You enchanted me, and I reached for your embrace. There, I found solace and life.

Your hand was soft as you fingered my brow and whispered assurances of safe passage. You looked into my soul and translated the language of my heart. You found your name repeated countless times in my being and understood the melodies that birthed each time your name echoed my mind's halls.

It is for you that I run to sleep, to dream of treasures and adventures to pursue and yet, I am all the more eager to wake to see dawn flood your face each morning. There is no natural sleep of this life that can keep me from you. You are my most sought-after punctuation of my life's expression—the pauses, the exclamations, the questions and even the joyful expletives. I am not your completion—I am your partner and we climb and descend together. Our eye is focused on the realities of tomorrow that we vision today. We smell its savor and marry the taste in our mouths. Our hands feel the tow of its bearing today.

Words diminish in talent while attempting to render the ecstasy I find in your presence. There is nothing in my past or shadow of unrealized dreams that dares exalt itself to our union. Thank you for allowing me to hold your hand.

For her,

When I . . .

When I was a younger man, the prize I sought and valued, from the softer gender, was passion . . .

and in time, fortunately, I had my fill.

Now wisdom, as ushered by time, has taught me what true worth is.

I now appreciate the treasure . . .

this treasure, I've received into outstretched hands . . . I cradle and care for it in both, lest I foil and drop this prize . . .

I hold the heart that loves me. I have entrusted her with mine.

I can only carefully hold one heart, although passion's heat sometimes seems insatiable . . .

If I am wise, I understand limits and *the dance,* while still appealing, is not always worth the experience at peril of failing my hand's grip.

Love Them

Monologue for Pastor Seedsmith in the stage play
"Broken Ground"

People are scared. Many live in fear daily. A lot are hurting with pain and sorrow that is sometimes greater than anything that we can comprehend or imagine. The point of their pain may seem insignificant to you or even trivial . . . but to them it's real . . . and it's theirs.

Please love them while they're hurting . . . love them more when they cry out, love them genuinely when they hold the tears inside. Try to understand, and if you can't . . . love them still . . . He still loves us.

Love them fiercely. Love them in the face of their enemies, in the face of their pain . . . hold on to them and don't let go, even if it kills the both of you. Love means giving all. Love hard, children! Love hard! Love real, not fake, not cheap, not convenient.

Love them until they own that demon, that adversity, that circumstance, that point of pain. Love them as if your life depended on it.

You, *Here*, Me
(for Kyra)

That place where you stood, you sat, you slept.
I have watched you,
Loved you, and cradled you in my arms.

Your bruises I've cleaned and chased waters
from your eyes.
I have watched you,
Loved you, and cradled you in my arms.

Taught your fingers, hands peeked and booed.
I have watched you,
Loved you, and cradled you in my arms.

Showed worlds, seen from shoulders, head and
back.

I have watched you,
Loved you, and cradled you in my arms.

Placed face in your hands, listened, gained instruction.
I have watched you,
Loved you, and cradled you in my arms.

Now you're a woman with child, loved and cherished.
I have watched you,
Loved you, and cradled you in my arms.

Teach her a parent's love, tried and proven
Because I have watched you,
And loved you, and will always cradle you in my arms.

your daddy

Perfect Man

There once was a perfect man,

That lived in the perfect house.

He did all the things he wanted to do,

And married the perfect spouse.

She gave him two perfect children

Who loved him and caused relief.

They never complained or expected

The things that would cause him grief.

This man of such perfect living

Could never stop from wanting more.

He struggled and strained without ceasing,

Till illness on him he wore.

This man now suffered in sickness,

His brow, now heavy in grief.

His time on the calendar marching

To that place were his life would cease.

His memory heightened in longing

For just plain and simple joys,

Of holding and having such pleasures

Of life, not things, his toys.

In truth, I know of no perfect people,

Nor families with perfect lives.

But I do know of grasps exceeding

The strength of imperfect drives.

Should time see us and this living

As wanton and wretch-less view,

Consider the viewpoint perspective.

Ask, if in time, this life is you.

Then, My Children

These then are my children.
Of all of them, I dreamed
Buoyed high in rushing waters,
Not debased by vengeful scream.

I dreamed my children visioned,
From slave ship and planter's row.
From terrors roped and beaten,
I knew the seed I'd sow.

Now time, the season beckons.
Harvest more creation pleas.
Spy I, my children dreamed for,
Clearly seen from timeless knees.

A Different Day

I didn't know if I'd ever see today—it seemed so distant, even unattainable but here it is; facing me, surrounding me and embracing me. This "is" my day and "is" is a very finite and definite place.

You know it's funny, I don't remember sending any invitations or preparing a guest list for consideration but "is" is here and now I understand that there is no escaping or retreat and what's more, there are no "do-overs".

"Is" has arrived, firmly anchored in this moment, having no need or desire for apology, exception, regret or any semblance of remorse.

Furthermore, I am understanding that "is" did not require permission or my consent. I am realizing that "is" is a sojourner and has journeyed to meet me, steadfastly enduring whatever difficulties it was presented. "Is" persevered with diligence and deliberateness. "Is" was not and could not be dissuaded or turned aside.

I now know that "is" is for me having been ordered and pre-ordained from before my creation or thought. I believe that "is" knew me and became very familiar learning my ways, my habits and devices, long before I did. I believe that as "is" studied me he became assured of the harmony and melody he would add to my existence and "be-ing".

Now I realize that without my knowing or even understanding I prayed for and longed for "is". I joined my wills, my energies as well as my exhortations to an expectation of the arrival of "is". He became a fruit of my faith, a product of my belief and desire.

Today I embrace "is" and welcome him. He is a comfort, a safe place and passage. He is my friend and He "is" me.

When You Were Still A Dream

(to the woman of some man's desire)

At times when I'd sleep at night

When lights were dark and still was quiet,

I'd lay *embosomed* in thought

Holding on to the notion that you existed,

Not knowing where you were

Or who held your heart or imagination,

I cradled you in my spirit.

I spoke your name in my prayers.

I knew one day we'd meet.

I held on to you,

Refusing to relent or relinquish my grasp,

I defended that space, that seat

That was designed and fashion

Only for you; your throne, that station

That only you could rule.

I dreamt of you.

Seeing you from afar

And knew you not by name but by appointment;

Your title and prestige preceded you

And preparations began with others

As your stand-ins.

This is your time

And time waits for you.

Knowing that your purposes

Are predestined and ordained,

Measured in fruit-filled effect.

You are a Queen of noble birth

Joined before the worlds began,

Called to champion the causes of right.

You have in attendance my heart.

Command me as you have in my sleeping . . .

When you were still a dream.

Unbanned Soul

A little boy of

dreams and hopes,

Laid lying on the floor.

With pants laid down

and **circused** frown,

He spied behind the door.

No screams or cries

just wondered **whys,**

Came attending to his call.

His mom can't tell

he'd go to hell,

No arms to stay the whore.

His dad, the fight,

would come with light,

If true was told not kept.

So buried pain,

in time to wane,

To cradle fractured step.

In church house space,

he'd sought God's face,

He'd lain beyond the mark.

Of lusted sin,

he held within.

He thought t'was his own dark.

Came hurt to mend

and comprehend,

Pursued with slanted view.

No rejoin to prayer,

it lingers there.

And color to turn to blue.

A man now he,

through married sea

He hoped to find release.

Set free the bands,

held heart and hands.

Turn dreams at last to peace.

It happened, yes.

Held still in chest

Unfit, not good at life.

And yet he held.

Still captive;***celled.***

Prisonered, constrained in strife.

And of the man

that held his hand,

and turned his face to his?

That mirrored look.

Mere innocent took.

Replaced, divided, **schiz'd**

Alas comes time,

to loose the bind,

That bridled troubles sow.

Undo the yoke.

Re-man, not cloak!

Forgive, return to know.

Still how he asked?

Unlock the pass,

Un-gate the future, see?

Strong hand not kin,

help usher end,

The road at last to me.

No spirit, flesh,

His sent, behest,

to champion, help the fight.

Set free the sin.

Forgived and mend.

Unchained a soul to light.

This little boy.

I know his hell.

I see him all the time.

His grey head bald.

Reflected all.

His eyes now framed in lines.

Bid love he chose.

But not from those.

In heart, could not commute.

In death, he thought.

No coition caulked,

Healed clef, new budding fruit.

New man now stands.

More stronger than,

the child of former hurt.

The guilt made good.

Now understood.

The steel that comes from dirt.

Early, one Sunday morning, I had a dream. It moved me. It seems to have been a continuation of a dream that I had some years ago. As such, I thought it worth sharing. For the reader, I offer this piece for your judgment and consideration, not as a sermon, indictment, or challenge of your beliefs, but as a stimulus to some intimate thought.

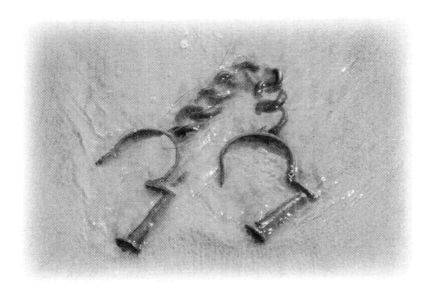

Dying Question

In this dream I had died, and, as such, I found myself before my redeemer, my Lord and friend. As odd as it might seem, the burning desire of my heart was to seek answers to questions that had puzzled and perplexed me over my lifetime. However, before I could speak, He put the following problem to me.

"If a person asks for my forgiveness, what do you think happens?" he asked calmly, as if genuinely wanting my input.

I looked into His eyes and saw honest concern and was disarmed. I responded, "You forgive him."

"Do you really believe that?" He continued, still in the tone of a pupil rather than a teacher.

I said, "Yes, you said all we have to do is ask from our heart, sincerely, penitently, honestly . . ."

"And what happens to the transgression, the error, the sin . . . the fault?" He returned.

"You forget it, it's covered, forgiven . . . and the debt is removed," I said, searching for the responses that came from my faith.

He looked at me and into me, not with condemnation, but with a loving sadness, and I became undone and naked.

I tried to cover myself, and I thought quickly and said, "You cast that sin into the sea of forgetfulness . . . you remove it from you as far as the East is from the West . . . you . . ."

He interrupted, "I do that?"

"Yes," I responded, less sure than before.

"Son . . . how do you forgive?" He asked softly, still wishing to learn from me.

The I got stuck in my throat, and I could not answer. It wasn't that I had lost the words or was ignorant of the answer, but shame and guilt wouldn't let me reply.

My mind swam as I thought of all the counter-arguments, defenses, and logic I could bring to bear in a debate with a man, but this was God, and my reasoning evaporated to mist.

I wanted to tell Him all the reasons that made it impossible for me to let go . . . tell Him about the hurt and pain . . . the memories and scars, but I knew He knew all these things already because He was there when they happened.

And before I could say it, He said, "You haven't forgiven me, have you?"

On this, a day of rejoicing and celebration, a day of homecoming, a day of finally talking with my King, face to face . . . my eyes were wet with tears, and I cried. I fell into His arms and He received me. He held me and showed His love through His embrace.

He said, "I understand; forgiveness is letting go. It's not holding you. You are holding it. Let it go because it has no grasp, no fist, no fingers, and no strength. The opposite of Love would have you believe that you can't let go. He would try to make you fearful of the "what ifs." Son, remember I am not a "What If." I AM! I am in control and nothing happens that I don't see and allow. You will understand the "whys" in time, and until then, be at peace and let go—forgive, just like I do."

When I awoke I was happy, shocked, and amazed. This was a very real dream to me, and it was like I had actually been talking with Jesus. It is with that same excitement that I offer this to those that need to hear it. Everybody may not believe this or understand, but someone will.

Now, this dream to me, by itself, seemed incomplete. It calls to mind many of the sermons and Sunday school lessons I heard throughout my years. The lessons our religious teachers advanced were great at encouraging control and abstinence and that has its place. However, sometimes the teachings did not include a "how to" beyond pray and believe. Please don't get me wrong; I don't disagree that we are encouraged and, yes, one might say, required, to forgive, but it would be helpful for our teachers and leaders to provide a functional approach for those of us for whom forgiveness is a real challenge. While we may know folks that simply can just forgive without a problem, for others it is more formidable. Perhaps they have tried with faithful obedience to exercise will and determination but have failed despite sincere and repeated efforts.

Before you consider me a heretic, please continue to read. It is not my desire to challenge or insult your faith, but rather to speak to the heart of believers that trust that we are not in this race alone or selfishly committed to our own well-being. We are more than our brother's keeper. We are family with one Father who says the world will know us by the love we show one another. Through our love, others may become aware and desirous of that same kind of connection.

Write the Vision (plain speech)

By the time I got to this part of my life, I was beaten up. I was more than messed up; a lot of stuff had whipped my butt. Nevertheless, standing up after being beaten down for so long was hard, but I still made the effort and stood. "Why me? Why's all this stuff happening to me?" I asked over and over, but no one answered. As I stood, I looked around and saw people with what seemed to be happy lives: happy families with loved ones, with people that cared. They seemed happy and successful. I decided I wanted to have what they had and began to try, but my hurts and the pains of my past stopped me. They seemed to laugh as if saying, *Who in the hell are you trying to fool? You can't do that.* These thoughts made me cry. I felt hurt and helpless. Knocked on my butt again, I heard a question in my heart. It seemed to ask if I really wanted to change my life—if I really wanted a life different from my past. In my mind, I responded, *Of course.* Then as I thought about it, I remembered all the people I blamed for my failures. I started counting and remembering. I thought, *If she had, or he had or hadn't . . .* Next, I remembered the abuses and would have continued to recount all the wrongs in my life, but then *Forgive* barged into my thoughts. I wanted to argue, to push the idea away, but it wouldn't leave. I couldn't answer. I didn't. *At least I'm alive and things really aren't that bad,* I debated. I wasn't drowning anymore, and at least I could watch people living the good life. Again, I briefly thought about changing my life and I realized I really didn't know if I wanted to. When the thought left, I felt sad and I experienced a sense of loss. In time, things started going bad again, and it became overwhelming. This time I felt like I was going to break. I wanted to give up. I broke down and cried aloud, "I DON'T KNOW HOW TO FORGIVE . . . HOW DO I LET GO OF THE PAIN?" I was breaking and on my way down, but before I felt the bottom, someone came after me and offered to help. When he offered help, we talked and I got to know him. He got to know me. I learned that I could trust him because he took time to build a friendship with me. I found out he had hurts, failings, endured setbacks and injuries too. In time, I came to understand that some were just like mine. He understood and didn't judge me. God's message to me, through my friend was simple, "Let me show you what I did".

When God brings us through crises, setbacks, and failures, often it is not punishment, as we may imagine. Instead, it may be for the benefit of someone's future struggle.

Is there someone you could help encourage, coach, or love through a challenge?

Share with that person how you conquered the greatest challenges of your life.

"Show" that man, woman, or child how you did it.

You may be the person with the key to their shackles.

Epilogue:
A New Vision

In a large room a chair lies on its side. It is not in the center of the room but lying near one of two doors in the room. The room is protected. Metal doors with wire woven reinforcements embedded within the small glass panels at eye level just above the door knobs further add to its impregnability. The doors are aligned on the opposite ends of the same wall. They open outward but are closed and locked.

This empty space is large and rectangular. It has high acoustic tiled ceilings with symmetrical alternating corrugated translucent light fixtures. Half the lights are on but since it is fully daylight, sunshine pours in through single rows of horizontal rectangle windows that border the tops of both the front and rear walls.

The pour of sunlight melded with the diffused fluorescent lighting made the space bright. This confluence of rays forced any lingering shadows to retreat and forage for hiding. The light illuminated the earth tones that adorned the space; the browns, oranges, yellows and reds were tasteful in an artsy, creative, and imaginative way and yet they seemed muted. The life in the colors seemed diminished.

Meanwhile, in the space there was that chair. It was wrong, alone, abandoned and broken. One of its legs was displaced, separated as if some trauma had caused an avulsion of this appendage.

In this moment, he asked, "what do you see?"

"I see a broken chair, out of place, 'un-righted', missing a leg", I responded.

"Why is that what you see?", he returned.

"Because it's damaged—out of place", I defended.

"Is there anything else in your view", he chided patiently.

"What do you mean?", I asked incredulously.

"What do you see?", he implored, "open your eyes wide, what is really in your sight?"

I felt ashamed and challenged and now I was reluctant to say anything. I continued to hesitate now feeling that I was being tested and that I had been moved, without my permission, to the role of a student and he now was exalted to become my teacher. I resented this reality and the thought annoyed me.

During this time, he had allowed the silence to continue without interruption but I was aware that my various facial demonstrations had been registered and marked.

Gently he reframed his question, "How do you perceive the space?"

"The space?" I retorted.

"Yes, the space", he returned unapologetically and without further explanation.

"The space . . . " I pondered aloud . . . "It is empty except for the broken chair . . . "

" . . . Empty?", he interrupted with an attitude of disbelief. "How can you say the space is empty? It is full, filled to capacity. How can you not perceive it?"

Feeling dumbfounded I choked back emotions that reinforced feelings of stupidity. I started several sentences, "I . . . cause . . . see . . . why . . . " but never would any additional words come to help express my thoughts that could explain my place, my position or my argument. I resigned and shrugged my shoulders in surrender and said, "I don't know"

He saw me and had compassion. After a look of understanding he spoke and used a term that was foreign and yet comforting.

He said, "Son, this space is full of life, the energy of souls permeate this place; merging, melding and passing through in agreement and peace. This is a good place!"

I looked at him in disbelief all the while wanting to believe. However, I paused, took in what he was saying and considered that he just might have some insight that I lacked.

"But how?" persisted and swam in my mind because I couldn't see what he described. Meanwhile, in his voice, there was a confidence and assurance . . . and he called me son. How had that happened, "Son?". We were not related. He was not my father, uncle, cousin or anything to me. Our occurrence at this place, in retrospect, appeared to be merely a coincidence but it also seemed that we had been summonsed—called into attendance—to view this space, which in and of itself bore no special significance or importance. It just was and we were here—called as if we were to witness something. "Why were we here?" was a question that was building within me and "because we were meant to be here?" seemed elusive and not wanting to be found. I considered posing my questions to "him" but quickly allayed that notion. I dismissed my query because I didn't want to delve down this tunnel of exploration. I imagined it would become more frustrating with many convolutions. Right now, at this moment it didn't seem worth the expense of energy.

So I returned to my original quest to obtain or at least gain insight to increase my vision—to see what he was seeing.

I asked, "How do you perceive the 'fullness' of this space?"

Without hesitation he said, "Let the 'light' come into your eyes—then see"

I nodded my head obligingly then uttered "uh-huh", feeling that his response was just as cryptic and nonsensical as ever. His response didn't sway me or move me closer to believe but I did believe that he believed and for that moment, that assurance gave me rest.

Time passed in silence and the moment was at ease and without tension. I looked into his eyes and saw sincerity and calm. His posture was at ease. Furthermore the confidence of his "be-ing" conflicted with the nothing-ness that occupied my gaze. There was nothing there. I saw nothing . . . the space was just as empty as I had first observed.

Wonder continued to fill me. I thought we were alone now this feeling that someone else was present further threatened to sever my cohesion with reality. Now i knew he really was seeing something and he spied the bewilderment in my face and said gently but distinctly, "Close your eyes."

I did obediently and then he touched my eyelids slightly and then said calmly to that someone else not seen, "open his eyes and let him see". He continued to speak to the unseen but my eyes remained closed. With my eyes closed, it seemed like hours but it was only a few seconds. Then I felt him lift his hands from my eyelids and say to me "open your eyes".

Immediately my eyes were overwhelmed by light, bright and almost blinding but then it softened and my eyes adjusted. Now, I saw life.

There was life all over. The colors on the walls that had afore appeared muted now were alive, moving, flowing, changing and reacting to an energy that I had not previously known.

As I continued to take it all in I became aware that this 'energy' was music, a melody, a rhythm, a chorus and an orchestration all at once. There were no speakers, no instruments but there were people or rather souls. Each soul harmonized and moved together; each different, unique but blended, some syncopated and yet in time, the same meter and the same key. The tempos rose and deceased and the moods and themes modulated but it was continuously fluid.

While I listened, I never heard any sad or sorrowful tunes, no dirges but occasionally there sounds of remembrance and nostalgia—and I guessed that in those notes there was a 'missing' but not sadness. I would use the word 'somber' to describe those tones but they were only brief movements that immediately lead to crescendos of joy and exuberance.

I became aware of something else with my new sight—texture. There was something palatable that I could sense, feel, experience and touch. It was like the comfort and softness of a warm blanket where no fear could penetrate. It was peace—peace that could be felt and swaddled.

As I turned my gaze back to him I saw that he was smiling and now his countenance had changed. He was luminous and music now ebbed from his being.

He took my hand and we moved down to the floor and I felt the souls of past lives brush against us, press us, and even move through us. The first time a soul moved through me it was disconcerting but not alarming. When I became aware that as they passed through me a part of their being was left inside me—deposited. The more it happened the more I was filled and as I filled I started to change. Lights of different colors began flowing from me and I became translucent and now I heard my own instrumentation chime and resonant in harmony with those around us.

In the next moment I realized that as my music was added to the chorus, the symphony, all the souls began to rise and the floor was no longer our boundary or limitation.

Souls took flight, flying through and around each other but also disappearing and reappearing through the vibrant colors on the walls. It seemed there had become a concert, a cooperation between the animate and the inanimate which defied all boundaries of logic and physics.

As time moved, the souls exited the space one by one leaving me and he as we had begun but we were not the same. I was changed and I 'saw' differently. Now as I inventoried the space, now devoid of the souls, I spied the chair upright and whole. It was now in the room's center. The chair had changed; it was fabulously and meticulously carved and adorned. It was ornately padded in an embossed with rich camel colored leather and gilded accoutrements. The chairs carved arms and legs were brazened and massive. The chair was regal and right—it was made whole and had become a throne of distinction.

Now the lighting of the room changed again and became natural. Sunlight again poured through the ceiling's high windows and the fluorescent lighting mixed adequately. However, there was a difference from before I had vision. The colors on the walls were still vibrant and the throne now was bathed in light. This chair now sat as important and positioned in a manner that made it seem bigger and even elevated. A platform had been built and it rested elevated from the floor. I moved in the space to change my perspective, to get a better look at the chair now mended and made whole. As I moved closer I realized that the chair indeed was larger as if it had grown—its dimensions and dynamics were transformed. I could see the platform that had been constructed in detail. It was beautiful and adorned to suit the throne that now sat atop of it. It was a noble place matched with a truly magnificent throne.

He said, "Why do you think the chair is a throne?"

I was startled, I had forgotten or lost track of the fact that he was still with me.

"How . . . ?" I began but silenced my thought to ask how he had known what I was thinking. I hadn't said it aloud, had I? I didn't recall but how did he know? In the moment I pushed the concern of his knowing aside.

"It looks like a throne, majestic, noble, detailed and unique but . . ." I trailed off suddenly feeling an advance of sadness.

"Continue" he said.

"I can't . . .", now feeling the wells of tears beginning to crest.

"What's making you sad?" he asked penetratingly. I sensed he was not going to allow me to evade or escape this move. His queen stood before my king and I felt I would fall unless . . .

"I'm sad because the chair was once broken and cast aside, now restored, even better than before, exalted and with distinction . . . but is empty . . . incomplete, unable to fulfill its purpose. A chair, a throne in and of itself can be an object of admiration—it's an artistic piece of furniture; ornate, decorated, embellished but inanimate and when empty—dysfunctional.

Its function is its true beauty and worth. It is destined to bear up, to support that person that bears the great weight of leadership. Thus the chair, the throne, must be strong.

As my thoughts continued to bounce against one another, to meld and then separate, he asked that infernal question again, "What do you see?"

After all this he is asking me again. I felt a surge of irritation swell in my core and I wanted to let it come forth but I subdued my passions by interjecting a thought of wonder and curiosity.

I remembered how my eyes had been unveiled before and the marvels I witnessed so I resigned myself to wait to see what would be revealed now. So with deliberation I considered his question again, widened my eyes and cleared my mind wanting nothing to block my perception.

Slowing I answered, "I see a throne vacant of its monarch."

"You see very well. I am proud of you. You seemed to have gained some insight" he chuckled.

I was happy and pleased that I had answered correctly but more important than my verbal affirmation was my cognitive consideration. I answered because I 'knew' the answer. I perceived it with all of my being and my soul resonated in agreement.

"Why is the throne vacant?" he enjoined my thoughts and made my confidence quake again.

In defense I uttered, "I don't know . . . who is he or she? . . . where are they? . . . why aren't they here? . . . was it one of souls that departed?"

I was puzzled and my face broadcasted my dismay. I wanted to form a question but I could not find the words. Every thought that arrived in my mind was rapidly engaged by a counter and the 'counter thoughts' consistently won . . . so nothing came out of my mouth. The look on my face froze with my mouth agape.

He said, "It's your throne, made for you . . . it's your place" and with that he removed himself as the other souls returned and gathered as if forming a royal court.

"I don't understand" I said but there was no reply. He didn't answer. He wasn't there. He had been my support, encourager and guide but now at this critical moment I couldn't find him.

Then a curious thing happened. The music started and the souls lit up and the chorus began, but this time it included words. They were I indistinct at first but as they continued I started to catch the repeating theme. Continuing it became clear it was a question in repetition. Over and over they were singing with celestial accompaniment the question.

"What do you see? What do you see? What do you see, son? What do you see?"

When I heard the chorus interject 'son' I looked hard and there he was standing in front of the throne. He was larger than the other souls. With one hand he reached and extended it towards me and with the other he directed the path to the throne.

I came down to him and took his hand. Still puzzled I whispered, "What does this mean?"

He released my hand, took the first step of the platform and announce in a strong clear voice that caused the music to cease.

"Everyman is given a throne and every man is given a kingdom. Choose wisely my son how you will rule. Power has been given to you to subdue and take dominion of your kingdom. Only you can decide to ascend these steps to assume your position, your post, and your assignment. This is the question to you my son. How will you answer?"